THE INTERNET BUSINESS

Simple course study on how to do profitable business online

I0465274

Written By;
Yekini Monsuru Abisoye
http://y2mread.com
admin@y2mread.com
http://amazon.com/author/y2mread
www.facebook.com/yekini.monsuru

THE INTERNET BUSINESS

Simple proven and profitable way to do business online.

Hello readers.

I know you must have attended many seminars and webinars in order to make money online, and we both know most seminar coordinators charges huge amount of money starting from $100 to $500 USD.

Now the question is, what have you gained from those seminars you have attended?

How many business opportunities did they exposed you to?

The reason for writing this E-book is to ensure that people can be able to start their own business even if they do not have huge amount of money to attend big seminars.

Also some people do not have the time to attend seminar and all they need is quality information.

I have packaged 2 programs in one E-book and you can choose whichever you prefer.

That sound interesting right?

Of course, yes it is.

The first part teaches on how you can do digital business online without stress, all you have to do is to know the basic and you are good to earn money from this program. you may be earning up to $1100 in a month or even more than that.

The second part teaches on how you can do physical business online without leaving your computer and you can make up to $800 in a month.

So how much is this invaluable E-book?

We want almost everybody to afford it so we are selling it at a ridiculous give away price.

Author

Yekini Monsuru A

admin@y2mread.com

SIMPLE PROVEN STUDY ON HOW TO DO PROFITABLE BUSINESS ONLINE

MONSURU YEKINI

INTERNET BUSINESS

TABLE OF CONTENTS

1.INTRODUCTION

You must have heard a lot of advert on Radio, newspaper, billboard on how to make money online, and the advert always encourage you to come for a seminar or webinar and at the end of the day, you will be charged a huge amount of money before you can have the information.

I wouldn't blame them because organizing seminars involve a lot of money and stress, so I decide to write this E-book to reduce the cost and stress in making money online.

This E-book covers two major areas on how to do business online and I divided it into two parts; PART A and PART B.

The part A covers the first course which Binary option trading WHILE part B covers online mini Importation Business. So we will be starting with the former.

I have made this E-book to be simple to read and easy to grab and I assure you of its easy understanding. We strongly advise you to follow the steps in this E-book without jumping any step.

If you do this correctly, then you are welcome to the Millionaire crib.

Should you have any questions or Issue, kindly mail admin@y2mread.com and you will be treated with loyalty and respect. Note that it may take up to 2-5 business days for your mail to be replied.

Disclaimer

Trading binary option is very risky, but we have devised a simple way in which you will make profit from it, we therefore recommend you not to trade yourself or ignore any step stated in this E-book.

WE are not in any form responsible for any lost of capital or investment due to carelessness and Ignorance.

2. BINARY OPTION TRADING

Binary option is the most profitable business online that millions have been making money from. It is far better than Forex and it also cover Forex in itself.

Binary option is simple and easy to know and does not have any complexity in it; even an illiterate can practice binary option.

What are Binary Options?
Binary Options are financial trading instruments.
They are estimates of underlying assets performance during a given time frame.

In options we trade **on** the market and not **in** the market like other trading methods, and thus the amount of psychological stress isn't expressed, as you are just predicting the **direction** of an **underlying asset's** movement for a **predetermined time frame**.

The Definition of Binary Options

- The word binary stands for *"having two parts"*. Generally speaking, all you need to do is predict either "Call" or "Put". BO trading has only two investment possibilities for you to predict and then choose between.

- One investment possibility is expressed when you predict that the price of the asset will rise, this type of investment is named **"Call" option**. The other possibility is presented when you predict that the price of the asset will fall, this type of investment is named **"Put" option**.

- Choosing an asset is the first step of your investment. For instance, if you have an interest in gold prices, you may choose to place a binary investment in gold. Obviously, the more familiar you're with the gold market the better your chances are of successfully predicting the fluctuations of gold prices.

What Assets Can Be Traded As Binary Options?

You can either trade with:

- **Indices** – Such as Dow Jones, FTSE, Nikkei and many more

- **Forex-** Combinations for all the major currencies such as USD, EUR, GBP ,JPY and AUD just to name a few

- **Commodities -** Gold, Silver, Oil, Corn, Coffee and several more

- **Stocks -** Over 50 of the biggest and most interesting companies in the world from a variety of industries are available in the Optec asset list, amongst them - Google, Deutsche Bank, Coca Cola and many more.

3. HOW TO TRADE BINARY OPTION

It is simple and so easy, follow these four steps
1. Select your asset e.g. EUR/USD,
2. Set your expiry time e.g. 10:30,
3. Determine the action/direction e.g. call or put
4. Click on the orange BUY button to finally execute your trade

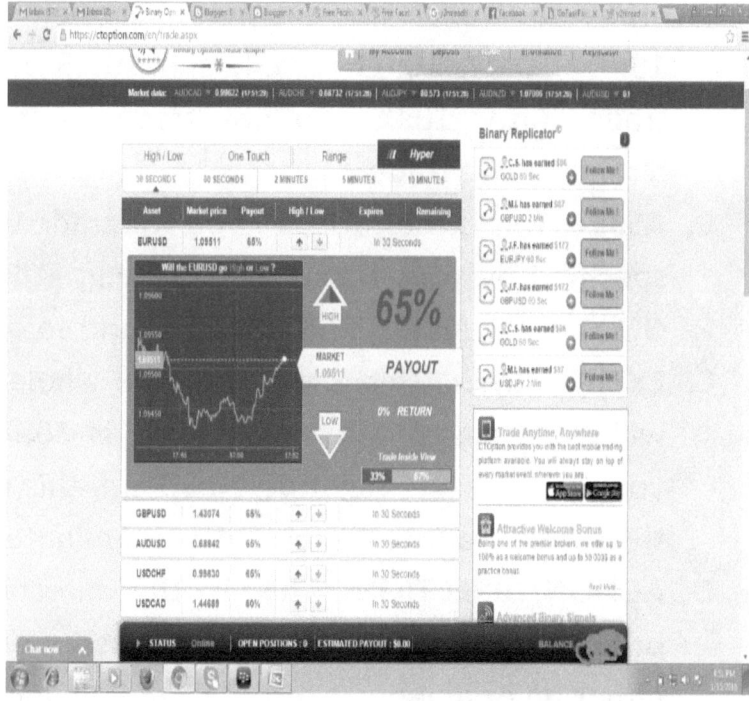

Let us explain each terminology.

A. Signal time: Signal time is the time you are expected to trade or enter a trade. It is very important to enter at the specified time frame, for example if your signal provider said you should enter a trade at 10:00 am, he/she is telling you that your signal time is 10:00 am, but most signal can be traded if the time frame from the signal time does not exceed 5 minutes. That is, if your signal time is 10:30, you have 5mins grace to trade, for example between 10:00. 10:01. 10:02, 10:03, 10:04, and 10:05 you can trade. After 10:05, do not trade again, it is already a late trade.

B. **ASSET:** This is the currency you will trade with as specified by your signal provider e.g. EUR/USD, GOLD, DAW JONES, and GBP/USD and so on.

C. **EXPIRY TIME:** This is the time the whole trade will close e.g. if your signal time is 10:00 am, your expiry time might be 10:30 am; this means the whole trade will expire after 30 minutes.

D. **ACTION/DIRECTION:** This is the direction or prediction where you think the asset will go, either up or down. E.g. up= call and down=put.

Can I Really Profit By Trading Binary Options?

Yes   **you**   **can!**

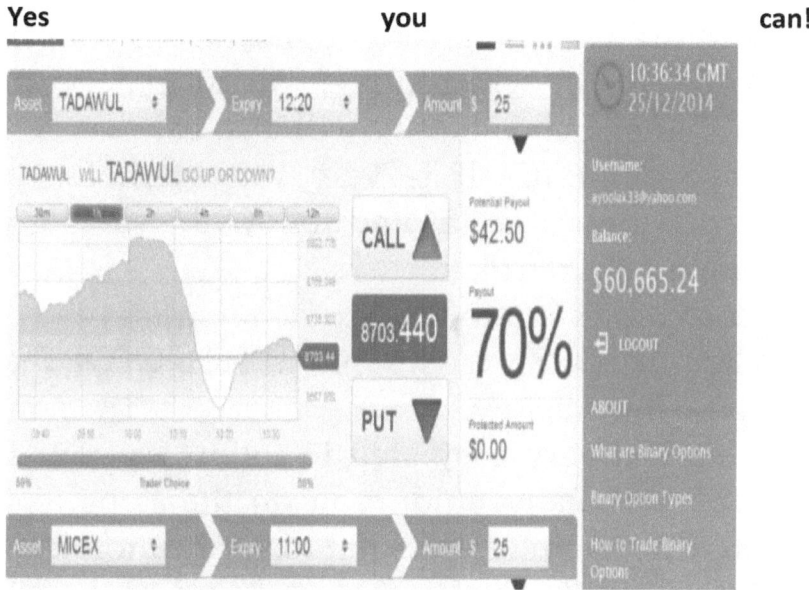

With consistent, regular and disciplined efforts, you can make handsome profits every day.

What Do I Need To Start Trading Binary Options?
- ✓ **Computer connected to the internet**
- ✓ **Broker's Account – www.bosscapital.com**
- ✓ **Minimum Investment Capital – $100, $250 depending on the Broker**
- ✓ **Signal Service –** www.y2mread.com/binarysignal

4. BINARY OPTION BROKERS

To trade binary option, you have to register with a broker, these broker works as your normal financial bank and help you to keep you money safe and secure for trading. You can make withdrawal whenever you like just as your bank.

Your broker will require you to make a deposit and after deposit, they will also ask you to verify your account. It is very important for you to verify your account and follow the steps given to you by your broker.

You can just go to www.binaryworldapp.com and click on OPEN ACCONT WITH CTOPT or use these links below.

This is a very easy step to follow as your broker will personally guide you on the steps to follow starting from Registration to verification.

Here are the list of Trusted and recommended brokers.

Press ctrl and click on the link below

CLICK HERE TO REGISTER WITH A U.S. BROKER; THEY ACCEPT PEOPLE WORLDWIDE, THEY ARE HIGHLY RECOMMENDED

CLICK HERE TO REGISTER WITH A NON U.S. BROKER; THEY DO NOT ACCEPT PEOPLE FROM U.S.A, BUT THEY ACCEPT PEOPLE FROM OTHER COUNTRIES

CLICK HERE TO REGISTER WITH ONLY UK BROKER, THEY DO NOT ACCEPT PEOPLE FROM OTHER COUNTRIES

CLICK HERE TO REGISTER WITH NON AFRICAN AND NON U.S. BROKER; THEY ACCEPT PEOPLE FROM OTHER COUNTRIES EXCEPT U.S.A AND AFRICA.

CLICK TO REGISTER WITH A FOREX BROKER; ONLY FOR FOREX TRADER

If you have any problem in registering, depositing and verifying your account with these aforementioned brokers, kindly send a mail to admin@y2mread.com

SAMPLE REGISTRATION FORM

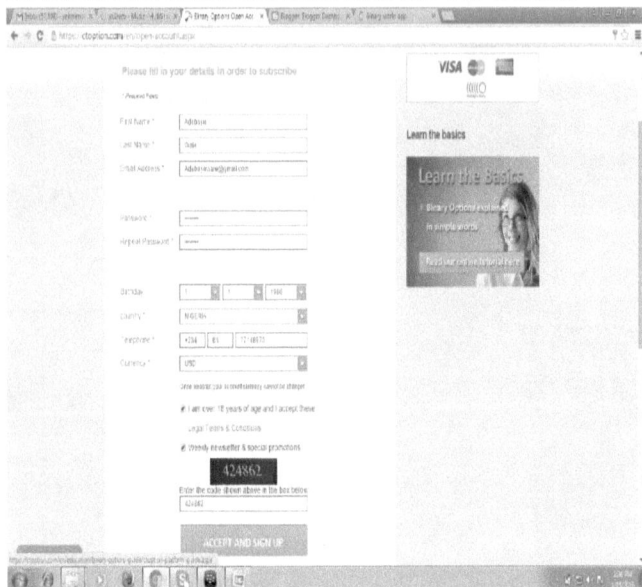

SAMPLE DEPOSIT FORM

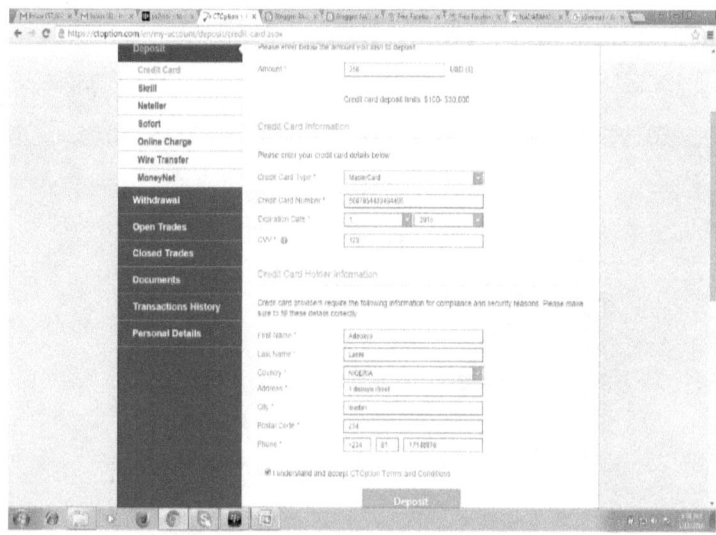

SAMPLE TRADING

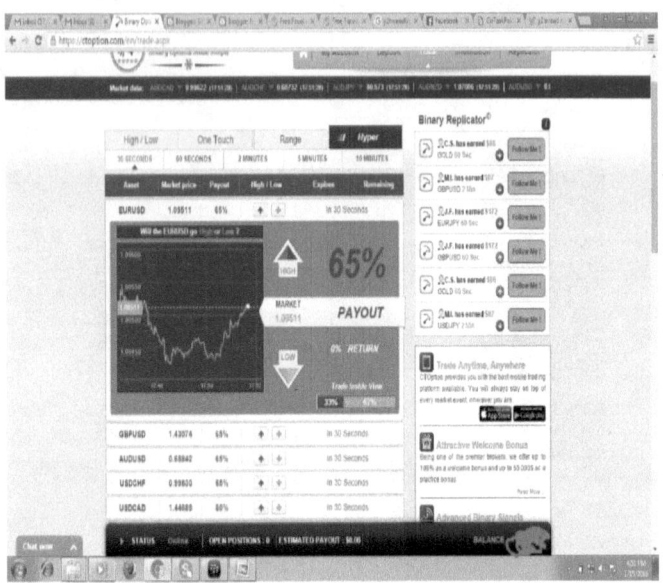

5. HOW TO MAKE PROFIT WITH BO: SIGNAL

In order to be successful in trading binary option, you have to trade with signals. Signal provider analyzes the market and provide signal for you in order to be successful.

We have partnered with one of these signal providers to deliver best result. To start receiving signals, you must have funded your account and ready to trade.

Go to http://y2mread.com/binarysignal and register for your signal.

HERE IS WHAT THE SIGNAL LOOK LIKE;

SIGNAL TIME: 10:00 am
ASSET: EUR/USD
EXPIRY TIME: 10:30 am
ACTION: CALL

Or may be as simple as this

10:00 am
EUR/USD
10:30 am
CALL

Allow me to explain each terminology.

E. **Signal time:** Signal time is the time you are expected to trade or enter a trade. It is very important to enter at the specified time frame, for example if your signal provider said you should enter a trade at 10:00 am, he/she is telling you that your signal time is 10:00 am, but most signal can be traded if the time frame from the signal time does not exceed 5 minutes. That is, if your signal time is 10:30, you have 5mins grace to trade. For example between 10:00. 10:01. 10:02, 10:03, 10:04, and 10:05 you can trade. After 10:05, do not trade again, it is already a late trade.

F.

G. **ASSET:** This is the currency you will trade with as specified by your signal provider e.g. EUR/USD, GOLD, DAW JONES, and GBP/USD and so on.

H. **EXPIRY TIME:** This is the time the whole trade will close e.g. if your signal time is 10:00 am, your expiry time might be 10:30 am; this means the whole trade will expire after 30 minutes.

I. **ACTION/DIRECTION:** This is the direction or prediction where you think the asset will go, either up or down. E.g. up= call and down=put.

Binary Options signals provide expert insights into market positions.

Signal Services help minimize investments risks.

They are mostly 80% - 85% accurate.

They are perfect for Short-Term Trades.

They are provided by professional expert traders. They are usually based on:

- Statistically Determined Current Price Patterns
- Market Trends
- Forex News and World Events

6. HOW TO WITHDRAW MONEY

To withdraw money from your account page with your broker is very simple, go to banking section and click on it. After you might have made the click, you will see a tab containing deposit and withdrawal. Click on the withdrawal tab and you will see your available balance and below it is a box container to input how much you want to withdraw. Note that you can only withdraw $200 directly into your debit/credit card, anything more than that will require wire transfer.

You must have done verification of your account before applying for withdrawal, contact your broker for more details about verification.

BY WIRE TRANSFER

BY CREDIT/DEBIT CARD

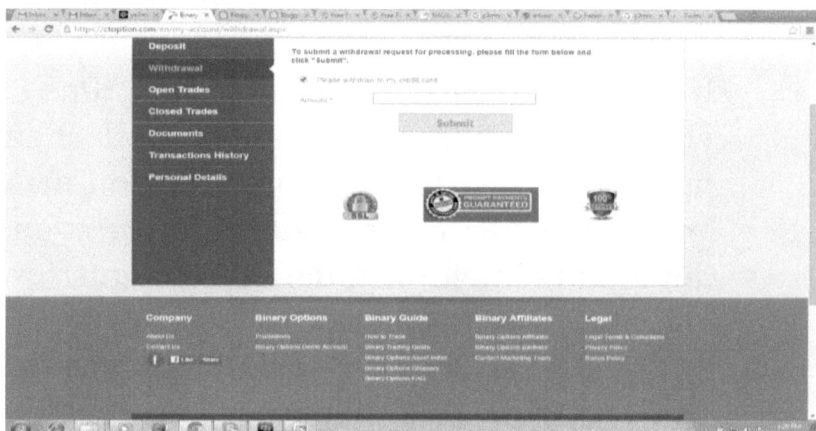

7. MONEY MANAGEMENT SECRET

1. *SET A DAILY EARNING TARGET FOR YOURSELF*

If your daily earning target is say, 50usd, once, you have made this amount, and then stop trading for the day. It is possible you make this amount in one trade, two trades or even more depending on your initial investments.

2. *DON'T INVEST MORE THAN 5% OF YOUR TOTAL FUND IN ANY GIVEN TRADE*

If your total fund is $200, then 5% is just $10
If you invest $10 in a winning trade, then payout is $18.5- $8.5 profit.
For 5 winning trades:
$8.5 X 5 trades = $42.5
In a week, you make $42.5 X 5 days = $212.5
In a month, you make $212.5 x 4 weeks = $850
Remove loses and errors of at most $200
Your balance is $550 in a month.
Traders trading with $20 will earn $1100 in month.

3. *DON'T INVEST WHAT YOU CAN'T LOOSE*

PART B
8. ONLINE MINI IMPORTATION

How to Start Your Own
Online Mini Importation Business
Even with little startup Capital

- **Market Research**

How do you know that people will buy what you're selling?
- **Product Sourcing**

Where do you find these cheap products that you can sell for high prices?
- **Payment Methods**

How do you pay securely for these products?
- **Shipment Methods**

How the products do get to you in Nigeria?

Selling Your Imported Products

➤ *Selling on Third Party Site*

➤ *Selling on Your Own Site*

➤ *Payment Processing*

➤ *Shipping*

➤ *Cash on delivery*

➤ *Selling Offline*

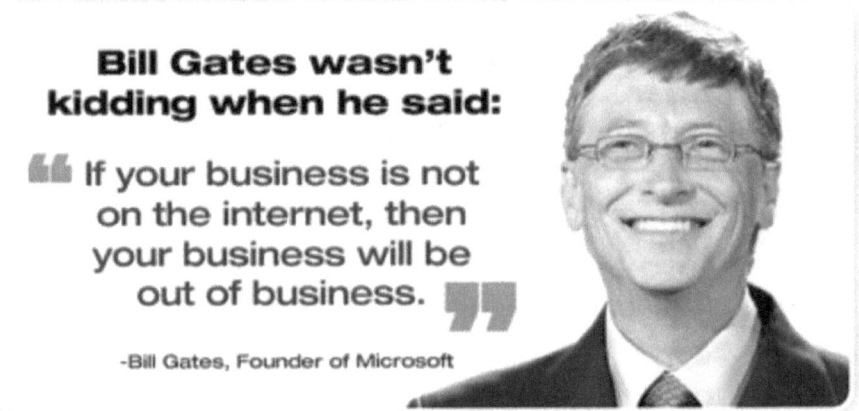

What you do NOT need to start online mini importation;

• Millions of naira as startup capital

• a shop or an office

- A license or all the obscure, difficult to secure paperwork.

- To travel to china, Dubai or USA.

9. MARKET RESEARCH AND PRODUCT SOURCING

How do you know that people will buy what you're selling?

"Give me six hours to chop down a tree and I will spend the **first four sharpening the axe.**"

Abraham Lincoln

ITEMS TO CONSIDER WHEN STARTING AN IMPORTING BUSINESS

- ✓ Small and light enough to be easily shipped

- ✓ Specific, niche products

- ✓ Consistent stream of buyers

- ✓ Selling for twice as much as your buying price

- ✓ Keep it in the $1-100 range

The BEST THINGS to sell are things that lots of people WANT, but not many other people are selling.

FOR STARTERS: DON'T

- ➤ go seasonal

- ➤ Sell what everyone else is selling

- ➤ Compete with established "Power sellers"

- ➤ Import fragile products requiring perfect shipping practices

- ➤ Sell stuff that nobody wants.

Where do you find these cheap products that you can sell for high prices?

Online sites you can order products cheaply

- **www.aliexpress.com**
- **alibaba.com**
- **1688.com**
- taobao.com
- saralovelyhome.com
- tigerdirect.com
- amazon.com
- tinydeal.com
- wholesalecentral.com
- dhgate.com

Payment Methods

MASTER CARD

VISA CARD

Shipment Methods

Courier:

Postal Services: **Nipost, USPS, China Post, Singapore Post**

10. STEPS IN BECOMING A MILLIONAIRE

Steps to Becoming a Millionaire In Less Than 10 Months

Step 1: Source For HOT Quality Products At Very Cheap Prices

Step 1: Source For HOT Quality Products At Very Cheap Prices

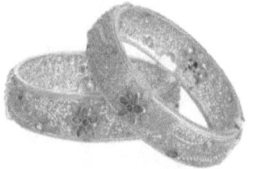

Kalyan Jewellery Gold San0010

Store No : 507009

ALEXANDER FASHION DESIGN CO.,LTD

TIPS

1. Use aliexpress.com

2. Use Mall4Africa.com

3. Search diligently for suppliers with great discounts

4. Use Free Shipping to reduce Costs.

Step 2: Sell Products At Not Less Than 200% Profit

At an exchange rate of 200 USD

Cost of one piece = **USD 0.398** == **=N=79.6**

Now let us compare the price with a Nigeria site which is konga.com

Step 2: Sell Products At Not Less Than 200% Profit

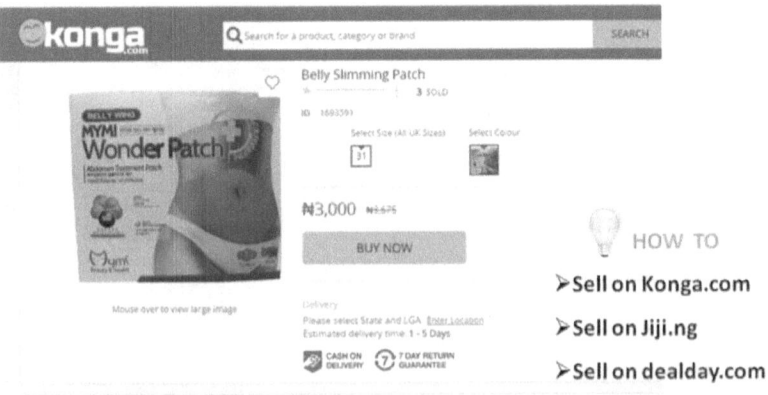

Profit on one piece = **=N= 2,920**

Step 3: Create Online Visibility for Your Store

- Share on facebook.com
- Share on twitter.com
- Advertise on Popular Nigerian Sites e.g. nairaland.com, jobberman.com etc

Step 3: Meet a Sales Target of Not Less Than 10 Pieces Per Week

- Total Profit per week = 2920 * 10 = 29, 200

- Total Profit in a month = 116, 800

- ==

- In 10 months,

   Accumulated Wealth = 116, 800 * 10 = **1, 168, 000**

11. REGISTRATION AND BUYING OF PRODUCTS

Step-by-step Guide on How to Register on Aliexpress.com

Step 1: Go to www. Aliexpress.com

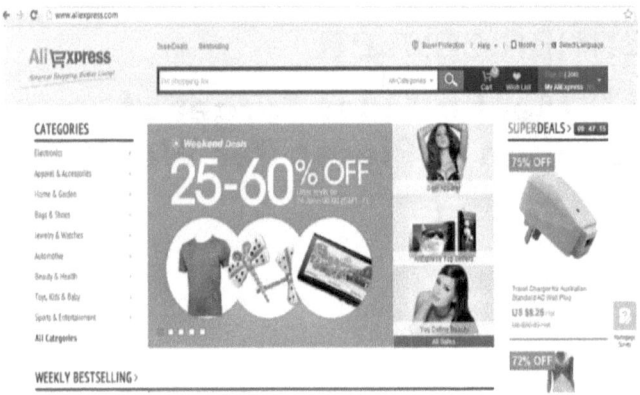

Step 2: Register on the site

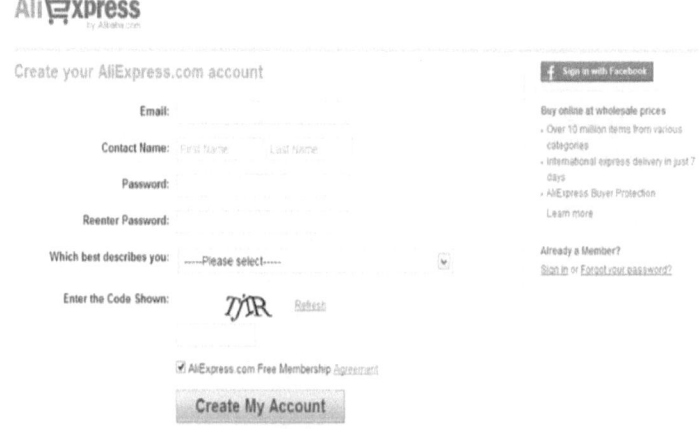

Step 3: Search for products

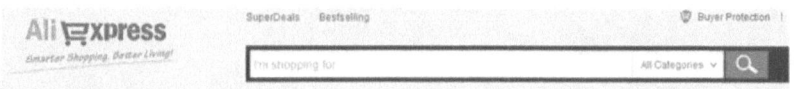

Search for any product of your choice, filter out paid shipping by click on free shipping at the far top of your search, and then click on the product to go to product details page. Check the feedback whether seller is a good seller or not, and select the quantities you want.

Product Ideas

- Health and Fitness products

- Adult Toys

- Car Products

- Beauty and Fashion products

- Consumer Electronics

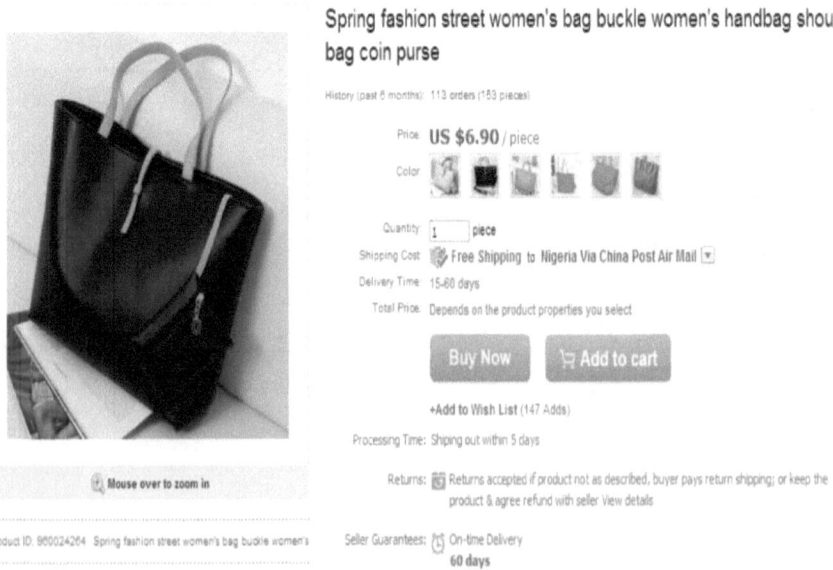

Spring fashion street women's bag buckle women's handbag shoulder bag coin purse

History (past 6 months): 113 orders (153 pieces)

Price: **US $6.90** / piece

Color:

Quantity: 1 piece

Shipping Cost: Free Shipping to Nigeria Via China Post Air Mail

Delivery Time: 15-80 days

Total Price: Depends on the product properties you select

Buy Now   **Add to cart**

+Add to Wish List (147 Adds)

Processing Time: Shiping out within 5 days

Returns: Returns accepted if product not as described, buyer pays return shipping; or keep the product & agree refund with seller View details

Seller Guarantees: On-time Delivery 60 days

Mouse over to zoom in

Product ID: 960024264 Spring fashion street women's bag buckle women's

Perfect quality cheap brazillian straight virgin hair

History (past 6 months) ★★★★★ Feedback (1) 1 order (3 pieces)

Price	US $0.01 - 171.00 / lot
	3 pieces - lot
Discount Price	US $0.01 - 153.90 / lot (11h 34m 34s)
Bulk Price	Additional 3% off (3 lots or more)
Stretched Length	

8 10 12	10 12 14	12 14 16	14 16 18
16 18 20	18 20 22	20 22 24	24 26 28
28 28 30	12 12 12	14 14 14	16 16 16	18 18 18

Quantity	1 lot
Shipping Cost	US $46.97 to Nigeria Via DHL
Delivery Time	4-8 days
Total Price	US $46.98

Buy Now   **Add to cart**

+Add to Wish List (5 Adds)

Processing Time: Shiping out within 3 days

Returns: Returns accepted if product not as described, buyer pays return shipping; or keep the

Product ID: 909521142 Perfect quality cheap brazilian straight virgin hair

0   0   +1   0

Qingdao Hot Hair Products Co., Ltd. (Depart...

China (Mainland) (Shandong)

96.7% Positive feedback

Detailed seller ratings (out of 5)

Item as Described: 4.4 Above Average
Communication: 4.7 Above Average
Shipping Speed: 4.7 Above Average

View my store ▸

· Contact Seller
   Contact Now
· Service Center
   Bella   Amy
   Neil   Kate

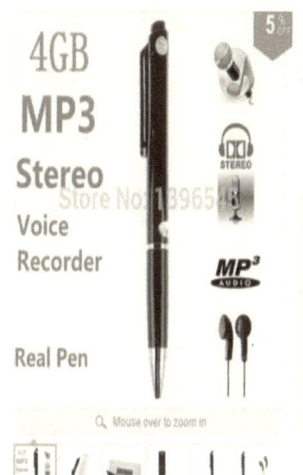

4GB Stereo USB Digital Spy Voice Audio Recorder Dictaphone Ball Pen MP3 64Hrs

★★★★★ **100.0%** of buyers enjoyed this product! (2 votes)   **7** orders

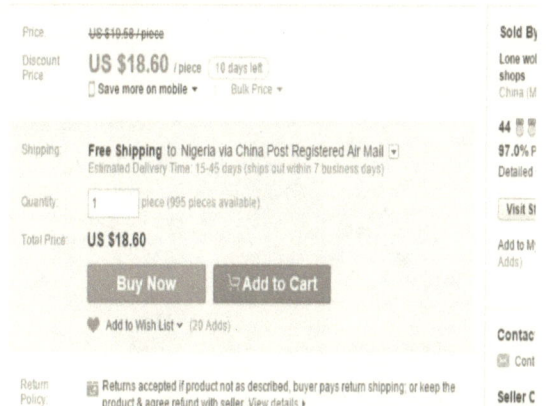

Price	US $19.58 / piece
Discount Price	US $18.60 / piece 10 days left
	Save more on mobile ▾ Bulk Price ▾
Shipping	Free Shipping to Nigeria via China Post Registered Air Mail ▾
	Estimated Delivery Time: 15-45 days (ships out within 7 business days)
Quantity	1 piece (995 pieces available)
Total Price	US $18.60

Buy Now   **Add to Cart**

♥ Add to Wish List ▾ (20 Adds)

Return Policy	Returns accepted if product not as described, buyer pays return shipping; or keep the product & agree refund with seller. View details ▸

Sold By

Lone wol shops
China (M

44
97.0% P
Detailed

Visit St

Add to M
Adds)

Contac
   Cont

Seller C

Sticky rat glue ,Strong stick rat board,big rats to stick ,MiceTraps

Price: **US $0.58** / lot

144 pieces / lot

Bulk Price: US $0.53 / lot (50 lots or more)

Quantity: 1 lot

Shipping Cost: US $26.32 to Nigeria Via DHL

Delivery Time: 4-8 days

Total Price: **US $26.90**

Buy Now   **Add to cart**

+Add to Wish List (1 Adds)

Processing Time: Shiping out within 60 days

Returns: No return necessary if product not as described, agree refund with seller. View details

Seller Guarantees: On-time Delivery
15 days

Mouse over to zoom in

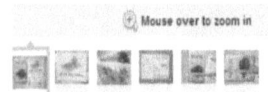

Transaction History & Feedback

4 transactions in last 6 months   Sort by latest

Buyer	Transaction Information	Feedback
C***a N.	US $155.00 x 1 Lot 07 Jun 2013 01:57	★★★★★ well recieved. thanks peter! Is this feedback helpful for you? Yes (0) No (1)
C***a N.	US $155.00 x 1 Lot 04 Jun 2013 04:59	★★★★★ the delivery was quick. thanks peter! you are a good seller. more orders for you. though am yet to confirm the durability and working status of the systems but i believe it is good. Is this feedback helpful for you? Yes (0) No (0)
O***o N.	US $155.00 x 1 Lot 20 May 2013 06:30	★★★★★ since am a new to this site aliexpress.com, dont have anything to say now until i receive and comfirm my product. Is this feedback helpful for you? Yes (0) No (1)
E***n N.	US $155.00 x 1 Lot 21 Jun 2013 07:26	☆☆☆☆☆ No feedback yet
K***o A.	US $155.00 x 1 Lot 19 Jun 2013 10:04	☆☆☆☆☆ No feedback yet

After selecting quantities, click on BUY NOW, and you will be taken to a page where to fill out a contact form. This is the name of the person, address, state, country and number to receive the product, Nigeria zip code is 234 by default, ignore the TEL NO and input your phone number without +234 in the Mobile number box.

Click on save to save the info, and then scroll down a little bit to click the continue/submit button.

You will now be taken to a payment secure page where you will make deposit with your debit/credit card.

Fill in the following details

Name on card,

Your card number (16 digits in front of your card),

Your card Expiration at the front of your card,

Your card CVV is the last three digits at the back of your card.

Click on pay now.

After this, if the payment is unsuccessful, call the phone number at the back of your card.

12.   TRACKING YOUR PRODUCT

Go to your profile icon at the far top left of aliexpress homepage after you sign in. Hover or click on it and select my order from the drop down, you will see lists of product you have purchased and added to cart.

Click on the product you have purchased that you want to track by clicking track order, you will see a 12 digits tracking code e.g. 1234767891NL and in front of it is the website to track it.

Copy the tracking number, click on the website link, and then paste the tracking link in a container box and finally click track.

Note that it will be easier for you to track by downloading 17track mobile app on iTunes or Google play store because it will enable you to track faster.

To check whether your product is in Nigeria, go to nipost.gov.ng and click on track international item, paste your tracking number in a box provided and click on track.

You will see the location of your goods.

13.   SELLING YOUR IMPORTED PRODUCT

After buying from aliexpress and you received the product, it is time to sell them online to make profit.

Selling on Third Party Site

Jumia.com.ng
0817 120 0277(Sam)

konga.com

dealdey.com
08090921463 (Olawale)

kaymu.com.ng
07080757766(Adebola)

Contact us if you need a Web shop,
admin@y2mread.com

Tranex-ng.com

ace.ng

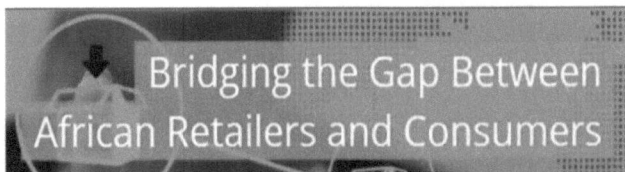

Facebook Marketing

Google SEO and adwords

Banner Ads
- Nairaland
- Lindaikeji
- Online Newspapers

OFFLINE METHODS

One: You can sell using a **FLIER**. Use www.canva.com to create a flier

Two: **AFFILIATE APPROACH**

Three: **RESELLER APPROACH**

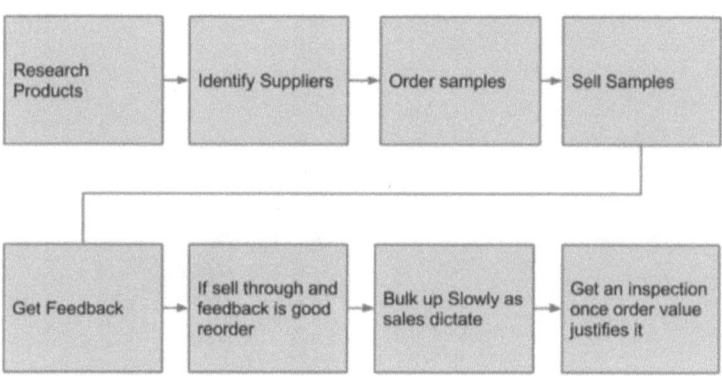

There are two mistakes one can make along the road to truth...not going all the way, and not starting.

Buddha

14. REGISTRATION AND SELLING

Go to www.konga.com/sell, click on register now, fill out the form as required, and submit. You will become a merchant.

After registration, login in into your seller account and click on SELL ITEM, you will be required to take a simple online test, after the test, you can start listing and selling your product.

If you have any question as regards your registration, mail us admin@y2mread.com

Selling on Third Party Site

Jumia.com.ng
0817 120 0277(Sam)

JUMIA

konga.com

dealdey.com
08090921463 (Olawale)

DealDey

kaymu.com.ng
07080757766(Adebola)

15. CONCLUSION

We have tried as much as possible to make the E-book comprehensive and also simple. We advised the reader to follow the step by step approach. If you have any difficulties, contact admin@y2mread.com.

Binary option trading is the fastest way to make money online and we encourage people to start with it and follow the step by step procedure.

Here are the list of Trusted and recommended brokers.

CLICK HERE TO REGISTER WITH A U.S. BROKER; THEY ACCEPT PEOPLE WORLDWIDE, THEY ARE HIGHLY RECOMMENDED

CLICK HERE TO REGISTER WITH A NON U.S. BROKER; THEY DO NOT ACCEPT PEOPLE FROM U.S.A, BUT THEY ACCEPT PEOPLE FROM OTHER COUNTRIES

CLICK HERE TO REGISTER WITH ONLY UK BROKER, THEY DO NOT ACCEPT PEOPLE FROM OTHER COUNTRIES

CLICK HERE TO REGISTER WITH NON AFRICAN AND NON U.S. BROKER; THEY ACCEPT PEOPLE FROM OTHER COUNTRIES EXCEPT U.S.A AND AFRICA.

CLICK TO REGISTER WITH A FOREX BROKER; ONLY FOR FOREX TRADER

Thanks,
Yekini Monsuru Abisoye,
http://y2mread.com

www.ingramcontent.com/pod-product-compliance
Lightning Source LLC
Chambersburg PA
CBHW021048180526
45163CB00005B/2339